Donated in honor of
Lauren Veitch
by Lance & Austin Waldrop
through the Friends of the
Library Matching Gift Program 2008

Pebble®

Caring for the Earth

Let's Recycle!

RECYCLE

by Anne L. Mackenzie

Consulting Editor: Gail Saunders-Smith, PhD

Consultant: Kate M. Krebs
Executive Director, National Recycling Coalition, Inc.

Capstone
press®
Mankato, Minnesota

Pebble Books are published by Capstone Press,
151 Good Counsel Drive, P.O. Box 669, Mankato, Minnesota 56002.
www.capstonepress.com

1 2 3 4 5 6 11 10 09 08 07 06

Library of Congress Cataloging-in-Publication Data
Mackenzie, Anne L.
    Let's recycle! / Anne L. Mackenzie.
    p. cm.—(Pebble Books. Caring for the earth)
    Summary: "Simple text and photographs describe recycling, why it is
    important, and simple ways children can recycle"—Provided by publisher.
    Includes bibliographical references and index.
    ISBN-13: 978-0-7368-6323-0 (hardcover)
    ISBN-10: 0-7368-6323-0 (hardcover)
    1. Recycling (Waste, etc.)—Juvenile literature. I. Title. II. Series.
TD794.5.M325 2007
363.72'82—dc22   2006005053

Note to Parents and Teachers

The Caring for the Earth set supports national science standards
related to conservation and environmental change. This book
describes and illustrates ways to recycle. The images support
early readers in understanding the text. The repetition of words
and phrases helps early readers learn new words. This book also
introduces early readers to subject-specific vocabulary words,
which are defined in the Glossary section. Early readers may
need assistance to read some words and to use the Table of
Contents, Glossary, Read More, Internet Sites, and Index sections
of the book.

Table of Contents

4

Too Much Garbage!

People throw away
garbage every day.
Some garbage goes
to landfills.
Many landfills
are filling up.

Jose and Jenny
throw away cans,
bottles, and paper.
Throwing away
these items is wasteful.

Recycling

Plastic bottles and other items can be recycled. Recycling makes new items from old items.

When people recycle, they help save trees, water, and energy. Many items people throw away are made from these resources.

At some factories,
used glass bottles are
made into new bottles.
Cans are melted into
car parts or new cans.

Jose learns to recycle.
He and his mom collect
milk jugs, cereal boxes,
and newspapers.

Jenny and her mom sort cans, bottles, and paper into recycling bins. They carry the bins to the curb.

Michelle looks for recycling arrows when she shops. Products that have these arrows are made with recycled items.

Caring for the Earth

When you recycle,
you help save
Earth's resources.
Let's recycle to take care
of the Earth!

Glossary

energy—power from coal, electricity, or other sources that makes heat and makes machines work

factory—a building where products are made in large numbers, often by machines

garbage—items you throw away because you do not need or want them anymore

landfill—an area of land where garbage is placed and then buried

resource—something valuable or useful to people and places; rocks, trees, water, land, and energy are some of Earth's resources.

wasteful—carelessly using up items and not thinking about saving them

Read More

Galko, Francine. *Earth Friends at Home.* Earth Friends. Chicago: Heinemann, 2004.

Green, Jen. *Waste and Recycling.* Precious Earth. North Mankato, Minn.: Chrysalis Education, 2004.

Internet Sites

FactHound offers a safe, fun way to find Internet sites related to this book. All of the sites on FactHound have been researched by our staff.

Here's how:

1. Visit *www.facthound.com*
2. Choose your grade level.
3. Type in this book ID **0736863230** for age-appropriate sites. You may also browse subjects by clicking on letters, or by clicking on pictures and words.
4. Click on the **Fetch It** button.

FactHound will fetch the best sites for you!

Index

Word Count: 154
Grade: 1
Early-Intervention Level: 15

Editorial Credits
Mari Schuh, editor; Juliette Peters, designer; Wanda Winch, photo researcher; Scott Thoms, photo editor

Photo Credits
Capstone Press/Karon Dubke, cover, 1, 6, 8 (both), 14, 16, 18
Creatas, 4
Image Ideas/Wallace Garrison, 10
PhotoEdit Inc./David Young-Wolff, 20; Robin Nelson, 12